A Note From Denise Renner

The Word of God is so powerful in our ~
It is essential that every person spend time
with God and study His Word in order to stay
spiritually strong in these last days.

This study guide corresponds to my *TIME With
Denise Renner* TV program by the same title
that can be viewed at **deniserenner.org**. My
desire is that through these lessons, you find the encouragement and freedom in Christ that you need. I believe the Holy Spirit is going to speak
to you through the words you read in this study tool and that as you begin
to use it, you will be *propelled* into the abundant life God has planned for
you. I encourage you to make the effort to receive all He has for you and
all He wants to do in you — it will definitely be worth it!

Whether you have walked with the Lord a long time or have just begun
to follow Him, there is so much He wants to give you from His Word. He
sees where you are, and He wants to meet you there.

> Therefore do not worry about tomorrow, for tomorrow
> will worry about its own things.
> Sufficient for the day is its own trouble.
> — Matthew 6:34

Your sister and friend in Jesus Christ,

Denise Renner

Walking in God's Will and Redeeming the Time

Copyright © 2024 by Denise Renner
1814 W. Tacoma St.
Broken Arrow, OK 74012-1406

Published by Rick Renner Ministries
www.renner.org

ISBN 13: 978-1-6675-0724-8

ISBN 13 eBook: 978-1-6675-0725-5

TOPIC
Knowing Who You Really Are

SCRIPTURES

1. **Ephesians 5:15-17** — See then that you walk circumspectly, not as fools but as wise, redeeming the time, because the days are evil. Therefore do not be unwise, but understand what the will of the Lord is.

2. **Exodus 3:1-5** — Now Moses was tending the flock of Jethro his father-in-law, the priest of Midian. And he led the flock to the back of the desert, and came to Horeb, the mountain of God. And the Angel of the Lord appeared to him in a flame of fire from the midst of a bush. So he looked, and behold, the bush was burning with fire, but the bush was not consumed. Then Moses said, "I will now turn aside and see this great sight, why the bush does not burn." So when the Lord saw that he turned aside to look, God called to him from the midst of the bush and said, "Moses, Moses!" And he said, "Here I am." Then He said, "Do not draw near this place. Take your sandals off your feet, for the place where you stand is holy ground."

3. **Hebrews 12:1** — Therefore we also, since we are surrounded by so great a cloud of witnesses, let us lay aside every weight, and the sin which so easily ensnares us....

4. **Ephesians 4:24** — And that you put on the new man which was created according to God, in true righteousness and holiness.

5. **Colossians 1:19** — For it pleased the Father that in Him all the fullness should dwell....

6. **Colossians 3:12** — Therefore, as the elect of God, holy and beloved, put on tender mercies, kindness, humility, meekness, longsuffering.

7. **2 Corinthians 5:17** — Therefore, if anyone is in Christ, he is a new creation; old things have passed away; behold, all things have become new.

8. **2 Corinthians 5:21** — For He made Him who knew no sin to be sin for us, that we might become the righteousness of God in Him.

9. **1 Corinthians 6:19** — Or do you not know that your body is the temple of the Holy Spirit who is in you, whom you have from God, and you are not your own?

10. **1 Corinthians 6:17** — But he who is joined to the Lord is one spirit with Him....

11. **Romans 5:5** — Now hope does not disappoint, because the love of God has been poured out in our hearts by the Holy Spirit who was given to us.

SYNOPSIS

Because of Jesus' sacrifice, there is no longer a veil that stands between you and God's presence. He so desires to be near you that He will make the first move in your direction and then invite you to respond to His love. You never have to question your worthiness because God has made you to be His holy ground — you stand completely blameless before Him in Christ! Hallelujah!

The emphasis of this lesson:

God doesn't want anything to stand between us and His presence. He demonstrated this when He instructed Moses to remove his sandals at the site of the burning bush. God also demonstrated this through Jesus' sacrifice, making a way for us to have unhindered access to His presence!

Understanding the Will of the Lord

As children of God, it is of utmost importance that we know and understand the will of the Lord for our lives. In Ephesians 5:15-17, Paul instructed us, "See then that you walk circumspectly, not as fools but as wise, redeeming the time, because the days are evil. Therefore do not be unwise, but understand what the will of the Lord is." According to this verse, one main way to walk in wisdom is to know and understand the will of the Lord. And the first step in knowing His will is understanding how He sees you — who He has created you to be. Once we understand how deep the Father's desire is for close fellowship with us, it's not hard to believe that He would go to such great lengths to redeem us — and redeem our time.

God Makes the First Move

Exodus 3:1-5 recounts the story of Moses encountering the holiness of God.

> **Now Moses was tending the flock of Jethro his father-in-law, the priest of Midian. And he led the flock to the back of the desert, and came to Horeb, the mountain of God. And the Angel of the Lord appeared to him in a flame of fire from the midst of a bush. So he looked, and behold, the bush was burning with fire, but the bush was not consumed. Then Moses said, "I will now turn aside and see this great sight, why the bush does not burn."**
>
> **So when the Lord saw that he turned aside to look, God called to him from the midst of the bush and said, "Moses, Moses!"**
>
> **And he said, "Here I am."**
>
> **Then He said, "Do not draw near this place. Take your sandals off your feet, for the place where you stand is holy ground."**

Moses was perplexed at seeing the burning bush because it was not being consumed by the fire. God captured Moses' attention with that miraculous fire, and when he turned to take a closer look, God made the first move by calling his name — and Moses responded with, "Here I am." Similarly, after Adam and Eve's sin in the Garden of Eden, they hid themselves from their Creator out of fear. But God made the first move toward them by calling out to Adam (*see* Genesis 3:8-10).

God also made the first move toward *us* when He sent His son Jesus to die in our place, and our acceptance of Jesus as Lord is how we respond to Him. God always makes the first move toward man. In John 15:16, Jesus says, "You did not choose Me, but I chose you and appointed you...." God chose us first and presents us with the opportunity to choose Him freely in return. God is *always* seeking after us.

The Fullness of God

We read in Exodus 3:5 that after calling out to Moses, God instructed him to remove the sandals from his feet. This is a very familiar passage of Scripture, and you may have read it before, thinking God was demanding respect and honor for the place where Moses stood — and that is likely part of it. But when you consider how God is always found seeking out closeness with man, you see that, really, God wanted Moses to experience the fullness of His holiness. He didn't want anything between them — not even a pair of sandals.

The same is true today. God does not want anything to stand between us and His presence or holiness, so God chose to become flesh and dwelt among us. He was born into this world clothed with human flesh, and He grew in wisdom, stature, and favor with God and man (*see* Luke 2:52). He went to the Cross, became sin for us, and redeemed us from the curse of the law, becoming a curse for us (*see* Galatians 3:13). He did all of that and more so we could have unhindered access to His presence.

The Veil of Separation

Before Jesus' sacrifice, no one besides the high priest was permitted to pass through the veil that led into the Holy of Holies, the innermost part of the temple where the presence of God dwelled. The priest was only allowed to enter once a year, not only to make an atonement for the people's sins but to do the same for his own.

Under the Old Covenant, it was not guaranteed that the priest or his sacrifice would be accepted by God, so the priest wore a robe with bells sewn into the bottom. The bells allowed those waiting outside the Holy of Holies to know whether the priest was still alive and whether God had accepted the sacrifice. One Jewish tradition says the priest also wore a rope tied around one ankle so that if the sound of bells was no longer heard, the rope would allow those outside to pull his body from the Holy of Holies.

The veil separating sinful man from the powerful presence of God is believed to have been several feet thick, and it was designed to fully hide the most precious place — the Holy of Holies. It was this veil that was torn in two from top to bottom when Jesus cried out from the Cross, "It is finished" (*see* Matthew 27:51, Mark 15:38, Luke 23:45, John 19:30). The barrier between the presence of God and man was *completely* destroyed.

You Are Holy Ground

So what does that mean for us today? Hebrews 12:1 says, "Therefore we also, since we are surrounded by so great a cloud of witnesses, let us lay aside every weight, and the sin which so easily ensnares us...." According to this verse, we must strip off, get rid of, and throw to the side every weight and sin in life that hinders us from experiencing all God has provided for us. Just as He did with Moses, God is inviting you into His presence. And just as God asked Moses to remove his sandals because His presence had made the place where Moses stood holy, God is asking you to lay hindrances to your spiritual walk aside because the Blood of Jesus has made *you* holy.

Ephesians 4:24 instructs us to "put on the new man which was created according to God, in true righteousness and holiness." When you were born again, God created a new spirit in you that is righteous and holy — *holy ground*. We must lay aside the weights and put on the new man — the newly created spirit — which is everything God's Word says we are in Him.

Colossians 1:19, 21, and 22 states, "For it pleased the Father that in Him all the fullness should dwell...And you, who once were alienated and enemies in your mind by wicked works, yet now He has reconciled in the body of His flesh through death, to present you holy, and blameless, and above reproach in His sight." We were once alienated from God in our minds because of wicked works. We were enemies, but we have since been reconciled to Him through His death, burial, and resurrection. Jesus' sacrifice made us holy and blameless, and we now stand before Him without fault!

In the original Greek, the word translated "blameless" in Colossians 1:19, 21, and 22 pictures someone standing before a court of justice, free from any accusation. According to Colossians 3:12, God sees you as "holy and beloved." *You are holy ground!* And since you are holy ground, you are also able to "put on tender mercies" because of the holy and righteous born-again spirit inside you. Because your spirit has been made holy, you now have within you the power that comes from God to be merciful and to extend kindness, humility, meekness, and longsuffering toward others — the same way He does!

Another magnificent statement about who we really are is found in Second Corinthians 5:17, which declares, "Therefore, if anyone is in Christ, he is a new creation; old things have passed away; behold, all things have become new." When we are born again, our previous life and its limitations have passed away. We are no longer that same person! We should not be identifying with our old selves by saying things like, "Well, I've always been an angry person" or, "I have a melancholy personality" or, "I am a bitter person and can't help it." No, the truth is, old things have passed away, and you are brand new on the inside!

One With Him

Second Corinthians 5:21 tells us, "For He made Him who knew no sin to be sin for us, that we might become the righteousness of God in Him." We can stand before God blameless because Jesus exchanged our nature of sin with His righteousness. In His humanity, Jesus was tempted in all the ways we are tempted, yet never sinned (*see* Hebrews 4:16). He was the spotless Lamb of God and willingly became sin for us so that in Him, we might become the righteousness of God. Jesus took the punishment upon Himself for every damnable thing we would ever think or do. In our born-again spirit, we are the righteousness of God, created in holiness.

First Corinthians 6:19 says, "…Do you not know that your body is the temple of the Holy Spirit who is in you, whom you have from God, and you are not your own?" Every inch of your body is the temple of the Holy Spirit. You carry the Holy Spirit inside you. Furthermore, First Corinthians 6:17 says, "But he who is joined to the Lord is one spirit with Him." If you were not holy and righteous on the inside, how could you be one spirit with Him? You couldn't be. It would be impossible!

But when you are born again, you *are* connected to Jesus, and you can have communion with Him because Jesus bridged the gap with His own blood and sacrifice. He brought you into communion and oneness with God. In your spirit, you are just as holy and righteous as He is! The very love of God — the love God has for Jesus — lives inside you (*see* Romans 5:5) and has transformed you from just an "old sinner saved by grace" into the righteousness of God in Christ! In these last days, it is vital that we understand His will for our lives by learning who He has created us to be in Him. This is one way we are able to redeem the time. And we'll talk more about that in the next lesson!

STUDY QUESTIONS

**Be diligent to present yourself approved to God, a worker
who does not need to be ashamed, rightly dividing the word of truth.
— 2 Timothy 2:15**

1. Jesus chose you; you did not choose Him. Read John 15:15-17 and explain in your own words what this passage means to you.

2. Read Genesis 3:1-13, Romans 5:8-10,18-20, and Second Corinthians 5:18-20. After Adam and Eve blatantly disobeyed God's command, who made the first move toward reconciliation? What was God's plan for reconciliation with mankind?

3. The veil separating the Holy of Holies from the rest of the temple was torn in two when Jesus cried, "It is finished." Read Luke 23:44-46, John 19:28-30, and Hebrews 10:19-22. What attitude or heart posture should we have when entering the presence of God? Why?

PRACTICAL APPLICATION

> But be doers of the word,
> and not hearers only, deceiving yourselves.
> — James 1:22

1. Read Hebrews 12:1 and 2 and examine your heart to determine if there are any "weights" coming between you and God. Ask the Holy Spirit to reveal anything you may be unaware of in your heart. Make a list of the first steps you can take *this week* toward laying those weights aside.

2. List one way you remember God "making the first move" in your life. Recount the story to yourself or share that testimony with someone you know who may need a reminder of God's love and desire for reconciliation.

3. Read Romans 5:5-8 and Colossians 3:12-17. Think of a person in your life to whom it may be difficult to show mercy, kindness, humility, meekness, and longsuffering. Ask the Holy Spirit for help in reflecting His character to that person and look for opportunities to love him or her with the love of God that has been shed abroad in your heart.

TOPIC

Knowing the Power of Forgiveness

SCRIPTURES

1. **Ephesians 5:15-17** — See then that you walk circumspectly, not as fools but as wise, redeeming the time, because the days are evil. Therefore do not be unwise, but understand what the will of the Lord is.

2. **Ephesians 4:31** — Let all bitterness, wrath, anger, clamor, and evil speaking be put away from you, with all malice.

3. **Proverbs 15:1** — A soft answer turns away wrath, but a harsh word stirs up anger.

4. **Matthew 6:11,12** — Give us this day our daily bread. And forgive us our debts, as we forgive our debtors.

5. **Mark 11:23-26** — For assuredly, I say to you, whoever says to this mountain, 'Be removed and be cast into the sea,' and does not doubt in his heart, but believes that those things he says will be done, he will have whatever he says. Therefore I say to you, whatever things you ask when you pray, believe that you receive them, and you will have them. And whenever you stand praying, if you have anything against anyone, forgive him, that your Father in heaven may also forgive you your trespasses. But if you do not forgive, neither will your Father in heaven forgive your trespasses.

6. **Matthew 18:23-34** — Therefore the kingdom of heaven is like a certain king who wanted to settle accounts with his servants. And when he had begun to settle accounts, one was brought to him who owed him ten thousand talents. But as he was not able to pay, his master commanded that he be sold, with his wife and children and all that he had, and that payment be made. The servant therefore fell down before him, saying, "Master, have patience with me, and I will pay you all." Then the master of that servant was moved with compassion, released him, and forgave him the debt. But that servant went out and found one of his fellow servants who owed him a hundred denarii; and he laid hands on him and took him by the throat, saying, "Pay me what you owe!" So his fellow servant fell down at his feet and begged

him, saying, "Have patience with me, and I will pay you all." And he would not, but went and threw him into prison till he should pay the debt. So when his fellow servants saw what had been done, they were very grieved, and came and told their master all that had been done. Then his master, after he had called him, said to him, "You wicked servant! I forgave you all that debt because you begged me. Should you not also have had compassion on your fellow servant, just as I had pity on you?" And his master was angry, and delivered him to the torturers until he should pay all that was due to him.

SYNOPSIS

One of the most powerful truths found in the Word of God is the power of forgiveness. Forgiveness is paramount to living a successful Christian life and redeeming the time that the enemy has stolen from us.

The emphasis of this lesson:

We must strive to forgive one another because unforgiveness can open the door to sickness in our physical body and torment in our soul. Jesus prayed, "Give us this day our daily bread and forgive us our debts as we forgive our debtors." Jesus has forgiven us all our wrongs, and because of that, we must also forgive those who have wronged us.

In the previous lesson, we learned that we are holy and righteous in our spirit. It is so important to meditate on these truths and believe what God has spoken. These truths are not just verses for us to memorize. We must understand that we have been given power from God through the Holy Spirit who lives inside us, which results in confidence and boldness in Him.

Ephesians 5:15-17 tells us, "See then that you walk circumspectly, not as fools but as wise, redeeming the time, because the days are evil. Therefore do not be unwise, but understand what the will of the Lord is." It is the Lord's will that we know who He has created us to be in Christ, but there is more He desires for us!

A Revelation of Forgiveness

The power of forgiveness is taught throughout the Word of God, but it is not enough that we merely think on or read about it. We must have a *revelation* of God's power of forgiveness and allow it to flow freely in our lives. We must strive to live with a forgiving attitude in our heart and extend that forgiveness toward others.

In the program, Denise shared this testimony from her own life:

> Many years ago, I struggled with forgiving others. For two years, I wrestled with unforgiveness, and as a result, I opened the door for the enemy to bring sickness into my physical body. For those two years, I also had painfully cold hands and feet without any relief. The battle went on for so long that great fear entered my mind, resulting in panic attacks. At that time, I didn't even know what a panic attack was. I was unaware that being under such tremendous pressure could affect a person's mind in that way.
>
> One day the Lord revealed to me that I had unforgiveness and bitterness in my heart that had allowed the enemy to wreak havoc on my soul and physical body. But when I chose to forgive, I was *absolutely free*! It was truly a miracle! The night that I made the choice to forgive the person who had hurt me, I went to bed sick in my body and tormented in my mind, but I woke up the next morning completely changed! I was totally healed in my body and completely delivered in my mind!

You Can Choose

The truth of Ephesians 4:31 is what brought about Denise's deliverance. "Let all bitterness, wrath, anger, clamor, and evil speaking be put away from you, with all malice." These instructions from Ephesians are not a suggestion — they are a *command*. This is the way God has called us to live.

As we walk through life, we will inevitably be wronged by someone at one time or another. Some people are so unhappy that it seems they carry within themselves the ability to stir up strife in all their relationships, which results in divisions between people. Have you ever been really hurt by someone and, even though you exercised forgiveness, thought, *I hope God deals with that person and reveals where he [or she] is wrong*? You may not realize it, but taking that attitude — even after you've decided to forgive — means you are allowing malice or evil in your heart toward that person. Ephesians 3:31 sets a much higher expectation and commands us not to allow this attitude into our heart.

Ephesians 4:32 describes the heart attitude we are commanded to carry: "And be kind to one another, tenderhearted, forgiving one another, even as God in Christ forgave you." After two years of fighting that physical and emotional battle, Denise had a decision to make. She could either ignore the Holy Spirit's promptings and continue in unforgiveness and bondage to the enemy, or she could redeem the time that unforgiveness had already stolen and choose to be kind, tenderhearted, and forgiving toward the person who had wronged her. And you have that very same decision to make any time you are met with wrongful treatment or strife.

God has already imparted kindness, tenderheartedness, and His very own love into your spirit, so that means your spirit already has the ability to be kind. When an attack comes your way, you can ruin the devil's plans by choosing to declare to your loving Father, "I know what that person did was hurtful and wrong, but I have You, the Greater One, on the inside. I have Your holiness on the inside. I choose to be kind and forgiving toward that person." When you make that decision, you are responding just as Jesus does — *and it is powerful!*

The Power in a Soft Answer

Proverbs 15:1 says, "A soft answer turns away wrath, but a harsh word stirs up anger." A soft answer has much more power than wrath. We live in a day in which many people believe that whoever yells the loudest will win the argument. There is a common attitude that says, "I will continue arguing until I prove my point. My opponent will eventually get tired of arguing and give up." This is not power, my friend. *True* power is being kind to someone who is mistreating you. *True* power is giving a soft answer from a peaceful spirit — and *that* is what will rebuke and silence wrath.

Again, Ephesians 4:32 says, "And be kind to one another, tenderhearted, forgiving one another, even as God in Christ forgave you." Sometimes, in order to be tenderhearted, we must speak to our heart and tell it what to do. We have to remind our heart that when someone says or does something hurtful, unkind, or demeaning, that person often does not realize he or she is being used by the devil to tempt us with offense.

One of the schemes the devil uses in the life of the believer is to tempt him or her to be offended. When offense enters the heart, it stops the perfect plan of God for that individual by causing him or her to stop running the divine race God has planned and potentially fall away from God altogether.

God's will is always for us to have an amazing life with Him, and we can miss out on that incredible plan if we do not learn to use the equipment God has provided for us to stay free from offense. Every child of God has power and grace on the inside to obey the command of God and be kind, tenderhearted, and forgiving toward others.

Forgiveness Is a Daily Decision

Do you do everything perfectly in your life? Is every thought in your mind right and pure? Do you always treat others as God intends for you to treat them? The answer to each one of these questions is *no*. But just as God extends His grace toward us when we fail, we must be willing to extend that same grace toward others.

According to the original Greek, the phrase "forgiving one another" found in Ephesians 4:32 would be better translated as "*gracing* one another." When someone offends us, our response should be to *grace* that person with mercy and forgiveness. If we sow judgment, we will reap judgment (*see* Matthew 7:1). But when we sow mercy toward others, we will reap mercy (*see* Galatians 6:7). And if we forgive others, we will be forgiven (*see* Matthew 6:14).

Have you ever been cut off in traffic? Has a server at a restaurant ever spoken rudely to you? Has a loved one ever said something hurtful? There are many opportunities each day to yield to offense. In Matthew 6:11 and 12, Jesus prayed, "Give us this day our *daily* bread. And forgive us our debts, as we forgive our debtors." Notice the word "daily." Jesus instructs us to forgive in the same way we have been forgiven by Him, and according to this verse, we need to forgive *daily*.

God knew that we would not be able to accomplish this act of daily forgiveness in our own strength, so by His Spirit, He poured into our hearts His love (*see* Romans 5:5) — love that is not easily offended (*see* 1 Corinthians 13:5 *AMPC*). If you are born again, God's love lives inside you. It is not a smaller or lesser version of His love; it is the same love with which the Father loved Jesus — and you can operate from the power of that love in forgiveness toward others.

The way we operate from that power and deal with offense is to say, "God, I'm not going to hold on to that offense. I forgive the person who offended me. I release that person by the power of forgiveness." When we do this, we are able to live in freedom and can redeem the time that living in unforgiveness and offense has stolen from us.

Forgive To Be Forgiven

Many Christians are familiar with Mark 11:23 and 24, which states, "For assuredly, I say to you, whoever says to this mountain, 'Be removed and be cast into the sea,' and does not doubt in his heart, but believes that those things he says will be done, he will have whatever he says. Therefore I say to you, whatever things you ask when you pray, believe that you receive them, and you will have them."

However, many do not continue with or think about verses 25 and 26, which say, "And whenever you stand praying, if you have anything against anyone, forgive him, that your Father in heaven may also forgive your trespasses. But if you do not forgive, neither will your Father in heaven forgive your trespasses." Jesus places tremendous importance on forgiveness!

The Unforgiving Servant

In Matthew 18:23-34, Jesus tells a powerful parable dealing with the subject of forgiveness. There was a king who wanted to bring all of his accounts up to date with his servants who had borrowed money. One of the king's debtors owed him millions of dollars by today's standards and had no way to repay the debt. The king ordered that the servant and his entire family be sold to pay the debt. This man was so distraught that he fell to his knees and begged his master to give him more time, promising to repay everything he owed. The king had mercy on the servant, released him, and forgave his debt.

After being forgiven, the man went to a fellow servant who owed him a day's wages, which was about a thousand dollars by today's standards. The forgiven man grabbed his fellow servant by the throat and demanded immediate payment for his debt. And just as the man had begged the king, this servant also begged for mercy, promising to repay his debt. But instead of extending mercy, the forgiven man had his fellow servant arrested and put in prison until his debt could be completely paid.

Other servants who had watched the entire incident were very upset and reported to the king all that had transpired. The king was very angry and said to the forgiven man, "I had compassion on you and forgave your debt. Why didn't you do the same for your fellow servant?" (*See* v. 32.) The king called him "wicked" and then had him thrown into prison until his entire debt was paid in full! The Bible says the man was turned over to the tormentors.

Before Denise chose to forgive the individual who had offended her, she was in such distress. She was tormented with sleepless nights, pain in her body, and fear in her mind all because she had allowed unforgiveness and bitterness into her heart. But when she finally let go of the unforgiveness and released the person who had hurt her, she was completely free!

Whenever you decide to open the door of forgiveness to whomever you need to forgive, you open the door of Heaven into your life. You open the door of Heaven into your relationships, mind, thoughts, and emotions. That is the power of forgiveness! If you desire to buy back the time that was lost because of unforgiveness, you do it by knowing it is the will of God to forgive and then actually forgiving those who have hurt or offended you.

True Forgiveness

True forgiveness is agreeing with the power and love of God that is on the inside and saying, "God, you forgave me of so much. If you had not forgiven me, I would be headed straight to hell for all eternity. But God, You have forgiven me, and now I have the power of Your love on the inside. And by my own will, I choose to forgive and set free that person who hurt me so deeply. Forgive them, Lord. I release them to you."

It is so important to understand the power of forgiveness. In these last days, God wants us to be strong and free. If time has been stolen from you through unforgiveness, and if you have been tormented and robbed of joy, peace, health, and relationships, this is your moment to redeem that time by the power of true forgiveness.

STUDY QUESTIONS

> Be diligent to present yourself approved to God, a worker
> who does not need to be ashamed, rightly dividing the word of truth.
> — 2 Timothy 2:15

1. In your own words, explain Proverbs 15:1, "A soft answer turns away wrath, but a harsh word stirs up anger."

2. Read Ephesians 4:29-32 and explain what it means to be tenderhearted.

3. According to the original Greek writing, what is a better way to translate the phrase "forgiving one another" (Ephesians 4:32)?

PRACTICAL APPLICATION

> But be doers of the word,
> and not hearers only, deceiving yourselves.
> — James 1:22

1. Recount a time in your life when someone wronged you. Have you forgiven that person? If so, describe how the Lord helped you do that. If not, take time today to pray and ask the Holy Spirit to help you release that person and forgive.

2. Because forgiveness is something that must be done daily, we must always be prepared to forgive. Write out a short prayer that expresses your determination to exercise forgiveness toward anyone who may wrong you in the future. Then anytime you are presented with the opportunity to forgive, pray that prayer and move forward, not holding anything against anyone.

TOPIC

Knowing and Taking Advantage of Your Opportunities

SCRIPTURES

1. **Ephesians 5:15-17** — See then that you walk circumspectly, not as fools but as wise, redeeming the time, because the days are evil. Therefore do not be unwise, but understand what the will of the Lord is.

2. **Luke 15:11-32** — Then He said: "A certain man had two sons. And the younger of them said to *his* father, 'Father, give me the portion of goods that falls to me.' So he divided to them his livelihood. And not many days after, the younger son gathered all together, journeyed to a far country, and there wasted his possessions with prodigal living. But when he had spent all, there arose a severe famine in that land, and he began to be in want. Then he went and joined himself to a citizen of that country, and he sent him into his fields to feed swine. And he would gladly have filled his stomach with the pods that the swine ate, and no one gave him anything. But when he came to himself, he said, 'How many of my father's hired servants have bread enough and to spare, and I perish with hunger! I will arise and go to my father, and will say to him, "Father, I have sinned against heaven and before you, and I am no longer worthy to be called your son. Make me like one of your hired servants."' And he arose and came to his father. But when he was still a great way off, his father saw him and had compassion, and ran and fell on his neck and kissed him. And the son said to him, 'Father, I have sinned against heaven and in your sight, and am no longer worthy to be called your son.' But the father said to his servants, 'Bring out the best robe and put it on him, and put a ring on his hand and sandals on his feet. And bring the fatted calf here and kill it, and let us eat and be merry; for this my son was dead and is alive again; he was lost and is found.' And they began to be merry. Now his older son was in the field. And as he came and drew near to the house, he heard music and dancing. So he called one of the servants and asked what these things meant. And he said to him, 'Your brother has

come, and because he has received him safe and sound, your father has killed the fatted calf.' But he was angry and would not go in. Therefore his father came out and pleaded with him. So he answered and said to his father, 'Lo, these many years I have been serving you; I never transgressed your commandment at any time; and yet you never gave me a young goat, that I might make merry with my friends. But as soon as this son of yours came, who has devoured your livelihood with harlots, you killed the fatted calf for him.' And he said to him, 'Son, you are always with me, and all that I have is yours. It was right that we should make merry and be glad, for your brother was dead and is alive again, and was lost and is found.'"

SYNOPSIS

God gives us opportunities daily to receive the blessings of His presence, wisdom, peace, joy, direction, and provision in our lives. We must learn to recognize and take advantage of these opportunities to intimately know and be transformed by our Heavenly Father.

The emphasis of this lesson:

Jesus tells a notable story about two brothers and their very different relationships with their loving father. Each son had the opportunity to become more like his father, and each son missed and squandered his opportunity in his own way.

Taking Advantage of God's Opportunities

We have been studying the subject of redeeming time in our lives. Our key passage is Ephesians 5:15-17, which says, "See then that you walk circumspectly, not as fools but as wise, redeeming the time, because the days are evil. Therefore do not be unwise, but understand what the will of the Lord is." We have learned that there is power on the inside of every born-again believer that comes from knowing and exercising the will of God. We learned that because the love of God has been poured into our hearts, we have the power to be kind, tenderhearted, and forgiving toward those who have offended us.

In this lesson, we will focus on the topic of knowing about and taking advantage of opportunities given to us by God. If we are wise, we can receive many amazing blessings from God by responding to those opportunities correctly.

An Inheritance Too Soon

In Luke 15:11-31, Jesus tells the story of the prodigal son. He begins in verses 11 and 12 by saying, "…A certain man had two sons. And the younger of them said to his father, 'Father, give me the portion of goods that falls to me.' So he divided to them his livelihood." The younger son's request was disrespectful toward his father and very foolish. He was selfish and impatient and demanded his inheritance before its proper time.

Just imagine for a moment what must have been going through the younger son's mind once he received his inheritance. His pockets were filled with money, and he was probably thinking, "Now I can do whatever I want to do. I no longer need to listen to my father. I am free!" He took his money and traveled to a country far from his own, and in the process, found that he had wasted and spent his entire inheritance when an unexpected and severe famine arose (*see* vv. 14,15).

In Want

Verse 14 says the younger son "began to be in want." The original Greek meaning of the word translated as "want" indicates *desperation*. In other words, the boy was starving. If the boy's life were a candle, it would have only had a flicker remaining. He was barely surviving. Verse 15 continues, "Then he [the boy] went and joined himself to a citizen of that country, and he sent him into his fields to feed swine."

In that day, feeding the swine was the lowest job a person could possibly have. But this young boy was starving and so desperate that he was willing to accept that lowly position. In his starvation, if the boy had decided to eat any of the food he had been feeding to the swine, he would have been considered a thief and would have been beaten. He was, in essence, enslaved to the owner of the pigs.

Verse 16 says, "And he would gladly have filled his stomach with the pods that the swine ate, and no one gave him anything." The man who hired the boy cared nothing about him. He didn't even offer to feed the boy, even though he was starving. The boy's life was leaving him like the last flicker of a candle.

Reaping the Consequences

Verses 17-19 continue, "But when he came to himself, he said, 'How many of my father's hired servants have bread enough and to spare, and I perish with hunger! I will arise and go to my father, and will say to him, 'Father, I have sinned against heaven and before you, and I am no longer worthy to be called your son. Make me like one of your hired servants.'"

This young man realized he was starving; even his father's servants had more to eat than he did. In his mind, the son was rehearsing his speech to his father. When he "came to himself," he concluded that he was no longer even worthy to be called a son. This boy had missed his father's timing for receiving the inheritance because he was impatient. The boy was also arrogant, demanding his inheritance before its intended time.

Have you ever reaped the consequences of trying to make something happen instead of waiting on God's timing? We have probably all done this at one time or another. Similarly, we read in Genesis 16 about how Abraham, instead of waiting on God's fulfillment of the promise of a son with Sarah, tried to "help" God fulfill that promise by sleeping with Hagar. Abraham was given a son by Sarah's servant girl, but he was not Isaac, the son God promised.

Like Abraham, this younger son decided to do things his own way rather than wait for his father's plan. He traded life with his loving father for a life of slavery to his fleshly impulses and lack. The Bible does not specify how long this son spent in wasteful living, how long he had been starving, or how far he had to travel to get back home, but it does describe his father's unexpected reaction to his return.

The Father's Great Compassion

Verse 20 says of the son, "And he arose and came to his father. But when he was still a great way off, his father saw him and had compassion, and ran and fell on his neck and kissed him." Notice that it was not the son running to the father. It wasn't the son who laid his head on the shoulder of his father, nor was it the son who kissed his father. It was the *father* who welcomed his son with love and mercy! His compassion for his son was so deep that he was not moved by the appearance of his son or how he smelled, and he probably smelled like the pigs he had been tending. Even though the boy had left and lost the opportunity to get to know his father, his father remained unchanged in his love for his son.

The son admitted to his father that he had been wrong and that he felt he was no longer worthy to be called his father's son. What is remarkable is that the father brought up absolutely nothing about his son's mistakes, choices, or willingness to be a servant in his father's household. Instead, he did the unimaginable. Verses 22-24 state, "But the father said to his servants, 'Bring out the best robe and put it on him, and put a ring on his hand and sandals on his feet. And bring the fatted calf here and kill it, and let us eat and be merry; for this my son was dead and is alive again; he was lost and is found.' And they began to be merry."

The father instructed his servants to bring his own very best robe and put it on his son. He also asked his servants to put a ring on his son's finger and sandals on his feet. The robe represented the robe of righteousness, and the son was restored to standing without fault before his father. The ring represented authority. The father was demonstrating through the ring that he was reinstating his son's authority as his father's son. And the sandals for his son's feet were speaking, "Walk in what belongs to you. Let's go forward in this life together. There is no condemnation. You were as if dead but now you are alive! You were once lost and now you are found! Let's celebrate!"

The Angry Son

As the older son was coming in from the fields, he heard the sound of music and celebrating and asked one of the servants what was going on. When the servant explained that his younger brother had returned home and the celebration was in his honor, he became angry.

Verses 28-30 say, "But he was angry and would not go in. Therefore his father came out and pleaded with him. So he answered and said to his father, 'Lo, these many years I have been serving you; I never transgressed your commandment at any time; and yet you never gave me a young goat, that I might make merry with my friends. But as soon as this son of yours came, who has devoured your livelihood with harlots, you killed the fatted calf for him.'"

The older son had been with his father but missed the opportunity to learn from his father. The older son's heart was not like his father's. This son was unforgiving, bitter, fault-finding, and prideful. He accused his father, "For years I have slaved for you and done everything you asked me to do, but you never even gave me a goat so I could celebrate with my friends." This young man missed the opportunity to develop a compassionate, forgiving heart like his father's.

The Heart of the Father

Verses 31 and 32 conclude the story of the two brothers and their father. The father told his older son, "Son you are always with me, and all that I have is yours. It was right that we should make merry and be glad, for your brother was dead and is alive again and was lost and is found." Once again, the heart of the father is revealed.

Both of these brothers missed out on the many opportunities to learn from and understand the heart of their father. The younger son missed out by leaving home prematurely. He was impatient, arrogant, and wasteful, and rather than gleaning from his father's wisdom, he believed he knew better about his future. The older son was living with his father and had access to him and everything he owned, but the older son did not take the opportunity to reap from the wisdom his father possessed or develop a heart like his father's.

As children of God, we must not miss the opportunities we are given each day to demonstrate the heart of our Heavenly Father by exercising the same mercy He extends to us. We must recognize God's perfect plan and timing and not miss the opportunity to trust Him to bring His promises to pass. He is faithful!

STUDY QUESTIONS

Be diligent to present yourself approved to God, a worker who does not need to be ashamed, rightly dividing the word of truth.
— 2 Timothy 2:15

1. The younger son proved he did not know his father's heart when he said, "I am no longer worthy to be called your son. Make me like one of your hired servants" (Luke 15:19). What do Galatians 4:4-7 and Romans 8:15-17 say about our Heavenly Father's heart toward us?

2. Read Luke 15:20-24, Romans 5:8, and Ephesians 2:4-7. The prodigal son's father saw him when he was still far away. Explain the father's response and how it is similar to God's response toward us.

3. Read Luke 15:4-7 and Luke 15:1-32. Describe the similarities between these two parables.

PRACTICAL APPLICATION

But be doers of the word,
and not hearers only, deceiving yourselves.
— James 1:22

1. Read Ephesians 5:1 and First Corinthians 11:1. What is one attribute of your Heavenly Father you can glean from today?

2. Read Psalm 103:12, Romans 8:1, and Second Corinthians 5:19. The prodigal son's father didn't condemn his actions, but instead, celebrated his return home. Is there someone in your life who you pray will soon "return home"? Have you ever found yourself acting like the older brother in the story? Make the determination today not to hold that person's sins against him or her, but to pray for a quick return.

3. Was there a time in your life when you knew you had wasted an opportunity to know and imitate God? What mindset changes did you make to correct yourself? How did your life change after that correction?

LESSON 4

TOPIC

Knowing the Power of One Day

SCRIPTURES

1. **Ephesians 5:15-17** — See then that you walk circumspectly, not as fools but as wise, redeeming the time, because the days are evil. Therefore do not be unwise, but understand what the will of the Lord is.

2. **Matthew 6:11** — Give us this day our daily bread.

3. **Matthew 6:34** — Therefore do not worry about tomorrow, for tomorrow will worry about its own things. Sufficient for the day is its own trouble.

4. **Exodus 16:18** — So when they measured it by omers, he who gathered much had nothing left over, and he who gathered little had no lack. Every man had gathered according to each one's need.

5. **Lamentations 3:22-23** — Through the Lord's mercies we are not consumed, Because His compassions fail not. They are new every morning; great is Your faithfulness.

6. **John 21: 4-10** — But when the morning had now come, Jesus stood on the shore; yet the disciples did not know that it was Jesus. Then Jesus said to them, "Children, have you any food?" They answered Him, "No." And He said to them, "Cast the net on the right side of the boat, and you will find some." So they cast, and now they were not able to draw it in because of the multitude of fish. Therefore that disciple whom Jesus loved said to Peter, "It is the Lord!" Now when Simon Peter heard that it was the Lord, he put on his outer garment (for he had removed it), and plunged into the sea. But the other disciples came in the little boat (for they were not far from land, but about two hundred cubits), dragging the net with fish. Then, as soon as they had come to land, they saw a fire of coals there, and fish laid on it, and bread. Jesus said to them, "Bring some of the fish which you have just caught."

7. **John 21:14-17** — This is now the third time Jesus showed Himself to His disciples after He was raised from the dead. So when they had eaten breakfast, Jesus said to Simon Peter, "Simon, son of Jonah, do you love Me more than these?" He said to Him, "Yes, Lord; You know that I love You." He said to him, "Feed My lambs." He said to him again a second time, "Simon, son of Jonah, do you love Me?" He said to Him, "Yes, Lord; You know that I love You." He said to him, "Tend My sheep." He said to him the third time, "Simon, son of Jonah, do you love Me?" Peter was grieved because He said to him the third time, "Do you love Me?" And he said to Him, "Lord, You know all things; You know that I love You." Jesus said to him, "Feed My sheep.

SYNOPSIS

It is important to understand the power of *just* one day. If we do not understand this truth, our days will slip by without the expectation or recognition of the blessings God makes available to us. There is power in one day to see the blessings of God manifested in our lives!

The emphasis of this lesson:

We have been given one day at a time to live our lives, but giving in to worry allows the enemy to steal our days. It is of vital importance for us

to realize that God is a daily God with daily provision and blessings for us to receive.

We have been studying the importance of walking in God's will and buying back the time that has been stolen from us. We have learned that we must first know the will of God and then understand the power of forgiveness. We have also learned that we must be aware of the opportunities God has given us in our walk with Him.

In this lesson, we will focus on the topic of the power of one day. The key passage for this entire study is Ephesians 5:15-17 which says "See then that you walk circumspectly, not as fools but as wise, redeeming the time, because the days are evil. Therefore do not be unwise, but understand what the will of the Lord is."

The enemy will always try to steal our time and the good plan God has for our lives. But God has given us ways to redeem the time that has been stolen from us. One vital tool for redeeming stolen time is understanding the power of one day.

Do Not Worry About Tomorrow

In Matthew 6:34, Jesus says, "Therefore do not worry about tomorrow, for tomorrow will worry about its own things. Sufficient for the day is its own trouble."

Jesus stated very clearly that we are not to worry about the future. If there was anyone who could have worried about the future, it was Jesus. He knew that He was destined to be crucified and separated from His Heavenly Father, but Jesus never worried a single day of His life on earth.

In John 10:10, Jesus says, "The thief does not come except to steal, and to kill, and to destroy. I have come that they may have life, and that they may have it more abundantly." Jesus came to give us abundant life, and life is comprised of many days. He wants every day to be filled with His abundance, His presence, His joy, and His peace. All this is available to us every day — we must simply reach out and receive it by faith.

We are given one day at a time to live. If we spend it worrying about tomorrow or next week or next month or next year, we are allowing *today* to be stolen from us. There have been people who have nearly died prematurely but instead lived. After having this near-death experience, some have had dramatic changes in their attitudes, and instead of living with a negative mindset, they have become extremely grateful. Why? Because they didn't know if there would be more days ahead. Today is precious, and Jesus is exhorting us to not worry our days away.

The Bible says that as a man thinks in his heart, so is he (*see* Proverbs 23:7). If our thinking is, "Nothing good ever happens in my life," then that is exactly what we will get. But if we are looking up with expectant hope in our God, knowing He has given us an abundant salvation, we can expect many wonderful blessings today and every day.

Daily Bread

When Jesus prayed, "Give us this day our *daily* bread" in Matthew 6:11, He was emphasizing the importance of one day. We must develop an attitude of living one day at a time and remember that God has given us everything we need for today.

A helpful picture of this principle is found in the book of Exodus when God supernaturally provided the children of Israel with food while they were in the wilderness. God's provision was *daily*.

> **Then the children of Israel did so and gathered, some more, some less. So when they measured it by omers, he who gathered much had nothing left over, and he who gathered little had no lack. Every man had gathered according to each one's need. And Moses said, "Let no one leave any of it till morning." Notwithstanding they did not heed Moses. But some of them left part of it until morning, and it bred worms and stank. And Moses was angry with them. So they gathered it every morning, every man according to his need. And when the sun became hot, it melted.**
>
> **— Exodus 16:17-21**

Although Moses had instructed the people to gather only the amount of food they needed to eat for each day and nothing more, some did not listen to him and kept a portion for the next morning. In doing so, they were demonstrating worry. They were worried that God would not provide what they needed the next day. They did not believe that God is a daily God. How many of us today struggle with worry, wondering if God will supply tomorrow? God was saying to the children of Israel and to us, "I am giving you what you need for today and I want you to trust Me that I will provide everything you need for tomorrow."

Trust God for Today

Lamentations 3:22,23 says, "Through the Lord's mercies we are not consumed, because His compassions fail not. They are new every morning; great is Your faithfulness." God's compassions, His mercies, are new every morning. Each day He makes available to us His mercies anew. The compassions He is extending to you today are not the compassions of yesterday. The mercies for today are not recycled mercies from yesterday. They are brand new! We live in a day in which people are confronted with many temptations to worry, but if we will receive His compassions each day, worry will be stopped in its tracks and replaced with His perfect peace.

Provision for One Day

In John 21:1-19, we read a wonderful story about the power of one day. After Jesus had been crucified, buried, and resurrected from the dead, He spent a period of time on the earth showing Himself to His disciples and speaking peace to their hearts. The disciples had dedicated their lives to Jesus for three years, and now everything had changed. They were likely unsure how to move forward and wondering what to do with their lives.

One night, when several of the disciples were fishing in the Sea of Galilee, they found themselves working all night without catching a single fish. As morning approached, they heard someone from the shore telling them to put their nets into the water on the other side of the boat.

> **But when the morning had now come, Jesus stood on the shore; yet the disciples did not know that it was Jesus. Then Jesus said to them, "Children, have you any food?" They answered Him, "No." And He said to them, "Cast the net on the right side of the boat, and you will find some." So they cast, and now they were not able to draw it in because of the multitude of fish.**
> **—John 21:4-6**

The men then realized who it was who had called to them.

> **Therefore that disciple whom Jesus loved said to Peter, "It is the Lord!" Now when Simon Peter heard that it was the Lord, he**

put on his outer garment (for he had removed it), and plunged into the sea. But the other disciples came in the little boat (for they were not far from land, but about two hundred cubits), dragging the net with fish. Then, as soon as they had come to land, they saw a fire of coals there, and fish laid on it, and bread. Jesus said to them, "Bring some of the fish which you have just caught." Simon Peter went up and dragged the net to land, full of large fish, one hundred and fifty-three; and although there were so many, the net was not broken. Jesus said to them, "Come and eat breakfast." Yet none of the disciples dared ask Him, "Who are You?"— knowing that it was the Lord. Jesus then came and took the bread and gave it to them, and likewise the fish. This is now the third time Jesus showed Himself to His disciples after He was raised from the dead.

—John 21:7-14

After breakfast, Jesus asked Peter a powerful question — and He asked it three times.

So when they had eaten breakfast, Jesus said to Simon Peter, "Simon, son of Jonah, do you love Me more than these?" He [Peter] said to Him [Jesus], "Yes, Lord; You know that I love You." He said to him, "Feed My lambs." He said to him again a second time, "Simon, son of Jonah, do you love Me?" He said to Him, "Yes, Lord; You know that I love You." He said to him, "Tend My sheep." He said to him the third time, "Simon, son of Jonah, do you love Me?" Peter was grieved because He said to him the third time, "Do you love Me?" And he said to Him, "Lord, You know all things; You know that I love You." Jesus said to him, "Feed My sheep. Most assuredly, I say to you, when you were younger, you girded yourself and walked where you wished; but when you are old, you will stretch out your hands, and another will gird you and carry you where you do not wish." This He spoke, signifying by what death he would glorify God. And when He had spoken this, He said to him, "Follow Me."

—John 21:15-19

Consider the fact that this event took place *after* Peter had already denied the Lord three times. We cannot know for certain what was going through Peter's mind, but it was as if, in those three questions, Jesus was saying, "Peter, yes you denied Me three times, but it is time to get past this.

I have more for you to do than think about how you have failed." During this same conversation, Jesus shared with Peter how he one day would die.

In that one day, the disciples did not know they would see Jesus or that He would be preparing a meal for them. In that one day, the disciples who had not caught any fish all night, did not know they would haul in more fish than their nets were made to hold. In that one day, Peter didn't realize Jesus would restore his soul and open his eyes to his purpose.

The Power of One Day

Many years ago, as Denise was meditating on the story in John 21, the Lord said to her, "Denise, do not underestimate the power of one day because you do not know what I have for you in that one day. The disciples did not know they would see Me on that one day. They did not know they were going to have an amazing breakfast on that one day. They did not know they would have provision where they needed provision. Peter did not know his soul would be restored or know the manner of his death."

Another way to redeem time is by knowing the power of one day and not taking it for granted. It is important that we renew our minds to the power of 24 hours. God's plans for your life are good and not evil or for calamity. His plans are for a future, hope, and peace (*see* Jeremiah 29:11). Every single morning when you wake up, there is a provision of His compassions. As you begin a new day, just imagine the good things that God is ready to bless you with and embrace the power of one day.

STUDY QUESTIONS

Be diligent to present yourself approved to God, a worker who does not need to be ashamed, rightly dividing the word of truth.
— 2 Timothy 2:15

1. How does the power of one day relate to Psalm 30:5, which says, "...Weeping may endure for a night, but joy comes in the morning."
2. Read Luke 8:43-48. Explain how the power of one day changed the life of this woman who had suffered in her body for 12 years.
3. Read Luke 13:11-13. This woman had suffered for 18 years being bent over. In one moment on one day, she stood up straight. How does this story inspire you to stand with expectation for what God is able to do in one day in your life?

PRACTICAL APPLICATION

**But be doers of the word,
and not hearers only, deceiving yourselves.
—James 1:22**

1. Explain how worry tends to manifest itself in your life. Research and write down two scriptures you can use to combat worry.

2. Worry is a result of not trusting God. What does Matthew 6:34 mean to you, and how can you apply it to your life today?

3. If you have not been living your life understanding the power of one day, what steps can you take to change how you have been thinking?

   • Lifting your hands: Psalm 63:4 encourages, "Thus I will bless You while I live; I will lift up my hands in Your name."

   • Singing praises: Psalm 59:17 declares, "To You, O my Strength, I will sing praises; For God is my defense, My God of mercy."

   • Meditating on His Word: Psalm 1:2 reminds us, "But his delight is in the law of the Lord, And in His law he meditates day and night."

   • Giving thanks: First Chronicles 16:34 admonishes, "Oh, give thanks to the Lord, for He is good! For His mercy endures forever."

4. What can you do to give the Lord more of your time in worship? Could you get up a few minutes earlier each morning to spend time with Him? Why not take a minute to glorify Him right now?

LESSON 5

TOPIC

Knowing the Power of Being Thankful

SCRIPTURES

1. **Ephesians 5:15-17** — See then that you walk circumspectly, not as fools but as wise, redeeming the time, because the days are evil. Therefore do not be unwise, but understand what the will of the Lord is.

2. **Philippians 2:14,15** — Do all things without complaining and disputing, that you may become blameless and harmless, children of God without fault in the midst of a crooked and perverse generation, among whom you shine as lights in the world.

3. **Romans 1:20,21** — For since the creation of the world His invisible attributes are clearly seen, being understood by the things that are made, even His eternal power and Godhead, so that they are without excuse, because, although they knew God, they did not glorify Him as God, nor were thankful, but became futile in their thoughts, and their foolish hearts were darkened.

4. **Luke 17:13-17** — And they lifted up their voices and said, "Jesus, Master, have mercy on us!" So when He saw them, He said to them, "Go, show yourselves to the priests." And so it was that as they went, they were cleansed. And one of them, when he saw that he was healed, returned, and with a loud voice glorified God, and fell down on his face at His feet, giving Him thanks. And he was a Samaritan. So Jesus answered and said, "Were there not ten cleansed? But where are the nine?

5. **Daniel 5:23** — And you have lifted yourself up against the Lord of heaven. They have brought the vessels of His house before you, and you and your lords, your wives and your concubines, have drunk wine from them. And you have praised the gods of silver and gold, bronze and iron, wood and stone, which do not see or hear or know; and the God who holds your breath in His hand and owns all your ways, you have not glorified.

6. **Philippians 4:18** — Indeed I have all and abound. I am full, having received from Epaphroditus the things sent from you, a sweet-smelling aroma, an acceptable sacrifice, well pleasing to God.

SYNOPSIS

Thankfulness is one of the most important and powerful truths we can learn as children of God. If we do not maintain thankful hearts, our thoughts will become futile, and our hearts will become darkened.

The emphasis of this lesson:

Of the ten lepers whom Jesus healed, only one returned to thank Him. The healed man fell at Jesus' feet, expressing deep gratitude. As children of God and followers of Christ, it is important for us to develop a habit

of thanksgiving. There is great power in expressing gratitude toward God and others.

Thankfulness Redeems the Time We Have Lost

We have been studying how to redeem the time, which happens by knowing the will of God. Our key scripture is Ephesians 5:15-17, which says, "See then that you walk circumspectly, not as fools but as wise, redeeming the time, because the days are evil. Therefore do not be unwise, but understand what the will of the Lord is." The will of the Lord is to redeem time that has been stolen from our lives. If the enemy has tried to steal your joy, peace, or strength, the Lord desires that you redeem that time.

For example, time spent in bitterness or unforgiveness toward another person is precious time that can be redeemed through knowing it is God's will to forgive. Knowing there is power in one day can also be a way to redeem time. Maybe you have wasted your days not realizing all that God wants to do in your day. He has blessings to bestow and a purpose to fulfill through your life, but you must recognize the power of what God is able to do in one day.

A Thankful Heart Causes Us To Shine in the Darkness

Thankfulness is another way to redeem lost or wasted time. There is power in expressing thankfulness. Philippians 2:14 and 15 says, "Do all things without complaining and disputing, that you may become blameless and harmless, children of God without fault in the midst of a crooked and perverse generation, among whom you shine as lights in the world." When we maintain a thankful attitude and refrain from complaining, we shine.

You may find yourself in a situation surrounded by people who do not know God or understand your Christian values — they may even treat you badly. If you are surrounded by people who aren't saved, just remember that light shines best in the darkness. You shine with the light of the Gospel. If you are in the midst of people who do not appreciate you, don't hide your light — be thankful. Be thankful for the people you are surrounded by each day.

Denise told a story on the program of a time when she was in another country for several days for work. On the last day, a man approached her and said, "You are a mystery woman." She responded, "Well, I *am* a woman, but I don't know if I am a mystery." He continued, "My wife and I have been watching you for two days and you are *shining*!" As believers, we shine! Being thankful causes us to stand out in a crowd and shine forth His presence.

Futile Thoughts, Darkened Hearts

There is a verse in Romans concerning our qualities and characteristics — including thankfulness — and it is so powerful. Romans 1:20 and 21 says, "For since the creation of the world His invisible attributes are clearly seen, being understood by the things that are made, even His eternal power and Godhead, so that they are without excuse, because, although they knew God, they did not glorify Him as God, nor were thankful, but became futile in their thoughts, and their foolish hearts were darkened."

The beginning of becoming futile in our thoughts and darkened in our hearts is being unthankful. If we are complaining or being negative or argumentative, our minds become unfruitful, and our hearts become darkened. But thanksgiving is so powerful; it keeps our thoughts where they should be focused. When we complain by saying things like, "Bad things always seem to happen to me. God doesn't seem to hear me when I pray. Why do others always have good things happen and I never do? Nothing good ever goes my way," it causes our thoughts to be futile and leads to more emptiness and thinking the way the world thinks.

It is so refreshing when people express gratitude. Just as we appreciate gratitude, so does the Lord. When we say, "Lord, I thank You that I am alive today! I thank You that I have eyes to see and ears to hear. Thank You that I have legs to walk with and a mind to think with. Thank You that I have a home, a job, and food to eat. But most of all, thank You for my salvation, that You would choose me to know You and put Your Holy Spirit inside me! Thank You!"

Being thankful causes our thinking to be sound. But when we are not thankful, it causes our thoughts to be empty and our hearts to be filled with darkness. We need to maintain thankfulness and allow thanksgiving to flow from our heart and through our lips. There is power in thankfulness, and it brings stability to our hearts and minds.

The Thankfulness of One

Luke 17:11-19 recounts the story of ten lepers who encountered Jesus as He was passing through a village near Jerusalem. It was there that the ten lepers began to cry out to Him, "Jesus, Master, have mercy on us!" When Jesus saw them, He told them to show themselves to the priests to verify their healings, as was required by Levitical law (Leviticus 14:2). And as they walked away, they were healed!

Verses 15 and 16 describe what happened next: "And one of them, when he saw that he was healed, returned, and with a loud voice glorified God, and fell down on his face at His feet, giving Him thanks...." All ten lepers were healed, but just one of them returned to give thanks. The Lord notices when we are thankful, but He also notices when we are *un*thankful.

Verses 17 and 18 record Jesus' response to the one who came to give Him thanks, "Were there not ten cleansed? But where are the nine? Were there not any found who returned to give glory to God except this foreigner?" Jesus not only acknowledged this man's thankfulness; He also noted the nine who did not return to give glory to God for their healing. As this cleansed leper lay at Jesus' feet in deep gratitude, Jesus said to him, "Arise, go your way. Your faith has made you well" (v. 19).

Does Jesus notice when we have thankful hearts today? Yes. But does Jesus also notice when we are unthankful? Yes. It often seems we are tempted to keep asking Him for things. We may find ourselves saying things like, "Jesus, please bless my day...bless this...bless that," and we forget to give Him thanks. Our prayers should also include things like, "God, You are great and mighty! You are so wonderful in my life, and I love you, Father. Thank you for everything you are doing in my life. Thank you for helping me today. Thank you for the way you helped me last week and how you helped me yesterday. Thank you for helping my children and my family. Thank you for your great faithfulness in my life!"

God is so good and so amazing! He is just waiting for us to return to Him — like that one leper — and say, "Thank you!" As we give Him thanks, He pours back into us. We can never outgive God. As we pour ourselves out in thanksgiving, He will always pour back into us!

The Demise of King Belshazzar

Another example of someone with an unthankful heart is found in the Old Testament story about a very famous, powerful king who misused the gold and silver cups that had been taken from the temple of God. In Daniel 5:23, Daniel prophesied against the king and said, "And you have lifted yourself up against the Lord of heaven. They have brought the vessels of His house before you, and you and your lords, your wives and your concubines, have drunk wine from them. And you have praised the gods of silver and gold, bronze and iron, wood and stone, which do not see or hear or know; and the God who holds your breath in His hand and owns all your ways, you have not glorified." Belshazzar was killed that very night.

Denise shared on the program that when she read this passage, she said, "Oh, Lord, You hold my very breath in your hands, and You own all my ways. I will glorify You!" It is so important that we are thankful. We must allow that thanksgiving to flow from our heart and be upon our lips. There is power in expressing thanksgiving to our God who holds our breath in His hands and owns the paths of our lives.

I Am Full

The apostle Paul was a wonderful example of how we as believers should approach trials in life. Paul was in prison while writing the book of Philippians, and, according to scholars, the conditions of this prison were horrible. Paul was standing in raw sewage and was surrounded by death, yet he maintained a thankful heart. While in those appalling conditions, Paul wrote the words "joy" or "joyful" 19 times!

Philippians 4:18 reveals Paul's heart as he wrote, "Indeed I have all and abound. I am full, having received from Epaphroditus the things sent from you, a sweet-smelling aroma, an acceptable sacrifice, well pleasing to God." While in those horrendous conditions, Paul said, "I have all and abound. I am full…." Only a thankful heart could express this attitude. Gratitude produces supernatural joy, which is God's strength in us, despite the circumstances of our lives.

Thankfulness can even produce wholeness in your body. It can keep your mind sound in a world full of chaos and confusion. Thankfulness will also guard your heart from becoming darkened by depression or bad news.

Thanksgiving is a *powerful* tool we can use to redeem the time that the enemy has stolen from our lives!

In Ephesians 5:15-17, Paul exhorted us to walk wisely through this life, redeeming the time the enemy has stolen from us. We do this by understanding what the will of the Lord is, and His will is for us to know who we really are, to know the power of forgiveness, to know and take advantage of our opportunities, to know the power of one day, and to know the power of thankfulness.

STUDY QUESTIONS

Be diligent to present yourself approved to God, a worker
who does not need to be ashamed, rightly dividing the word of truth.
— 2 Timothy 2:15

1. First Thessalonians 5:16-18 says, "Rejoice always, pray without ceasing, in everything give thanks; for this is the will of God in Christ Jesus for you." Explain this passage in your own words.

2. In Philippians 4:6, Paul instructed us, "Be anxious for nothing, but in everything by prayer and supplication, with thanksgiving, let your requests be made known to God." Based on what you have learned in this teaching, why do you think Paul included the instruction to be thankful?

PRACTICAL APPLICATION

But be doers of the word,
and not hearers only, deceiving yourselves.
— James 1:22

1. Psalm 9:1 (*AMPC*) says, "I will praise You, O Lord, with my whole heart; I will show forth (recount and tell aloud) all Your marvelous works and wonderful deeds!" List five things you are thankful for.

2. Read Colossians 3:15 and think of an area of your life where you have not been letting the peace of God rule in your heart. Is it your health? Your finances? Your marriage or children? What is one thing you can be thankful for in this area?

CLAIM YOUR FREE RESOURCE!

As a way of introducing you further to the teaching ministry of Rick Renner, we would like to send you FREE of charge his teaching, "How To Receive a Miraculous Touch From God" on CD or as an MP3 download.

In His earthly ministry, Jesus commonly healed *all* who were sick of *all* their diseases. In this profound message, learn about the manifold dimensions of Christ's wisdom, goodness, power, and love toward all humanity who came to Him in faith with their needs.

☑ **YES, I want to receive Rick Renner's monthly teaching letter!**

Simply scan the QR code to claim this resource or go to:
renner.org/claim-your-free-offer

WITH US!